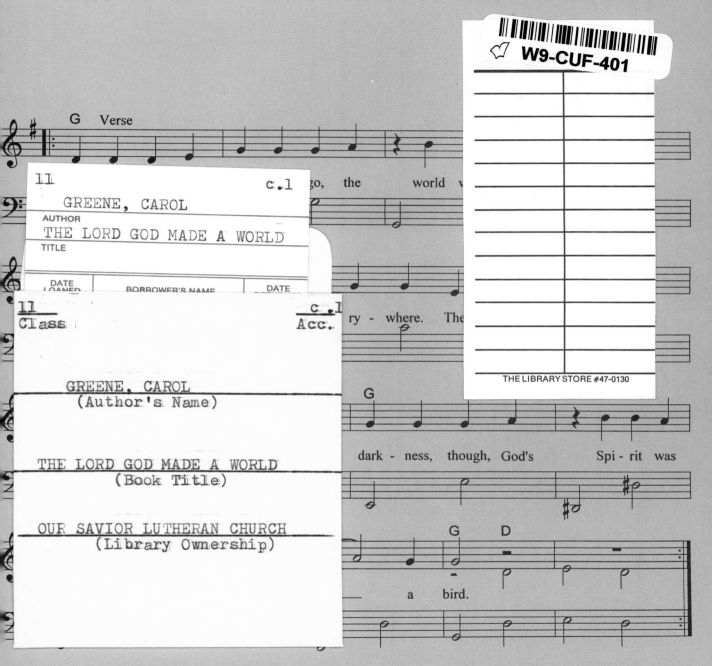

(Repeat chorus after as many verses as you choose.)

11   c.1
GREENE, CAROL
AUTHOR
THE LORD GOD MADE A WORLD
TITLE

DATE
LOANED   BORROWER'S NAME   DATE

11   c.1
Class   Acc.

GREENE, CAROL
(Author's Name)

THE LORD GOD MADE A WORLD
(Book Title)

OUR SAVIOR LUTHERAN CHURCH
(Library Ownership)

The Lord God Made A World

Carol Greene

Illustrated by Christopher Gray

The text of this book may be sung to the tune of "Do, Lord."

CPH
SAINT LOUIS

Sing hallelujah! The Lord God made a world.
Into the darkness His mighty Word He hurled.
And out of nothing creation He unfurled.
And God saw that it was good.

*L*ong ago, yes, long ago, the *(clap)*
    world wasn't here.
Darkness, darkness everywhere. The *(clap)*
    world wasn't here.
Even in the darkness, though, God's *(clap)*
    Spirit was near
And He hovered like a bird.

*O*n the first day of the week the *(clap)*
    Lord spoke the Word.
"Now let there be light," He said. The *(clap)*
    Lord spoke the Word.
"Light and darkness separate," He *(clap)*
    said, and they heard.
And God saw that it was good.

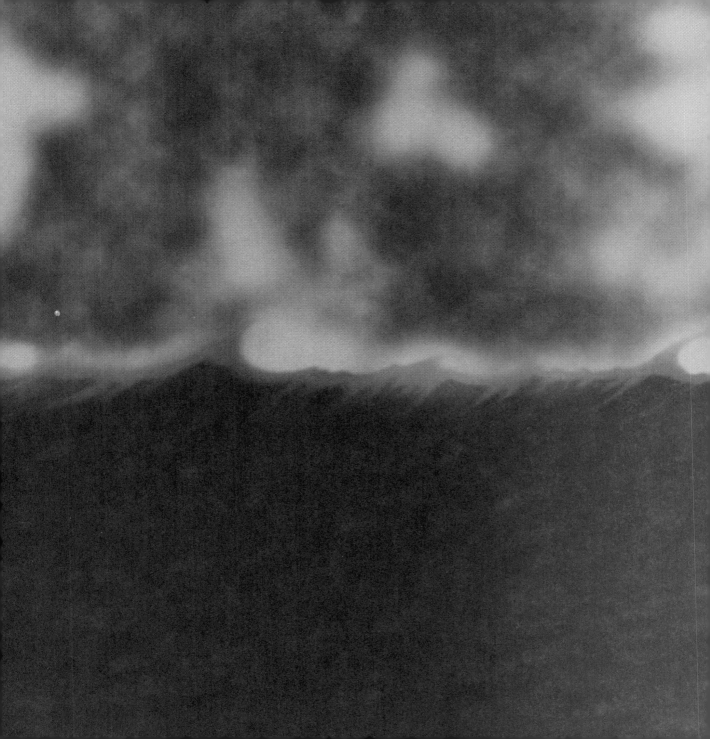

On the second day the Lord God *(clap)*
    spoke out again.
"Water go above, below," the *(clap)*
    Lord spoke again.
"In between the waters I will *(clap)*
    stretch out My heav'n."
And God saw that it was good.

*O*n the third day of the week God *(clap)*
    said, "Let there be
Seas and dry land on the earth." God *(clap)*
    said, "Let there be
Every kind of plant with seeds and *(clap)*
    fruit-bearing trees."
And God saw that it was good.

On the fourth day God divided *(clap)*
  daytime from night.
Then to shine upon His earth He *(clap)*
  gave each some light.
Day had sun and night had moon and *(clap)*
  stars burning bright.
And God saw that it was good.

On the fifth day God decided *(clap)*
    that He would make
Swimming creatures for each sea and *(clap)*
    river and lake;
Birds to fly across the sky and *(clap)*
    sing for His sake.
And God saw that it was good.

*O*n the sixth day God made all the *(clap)*
   creatures on land:
Cattle for the pastures; darting *(clap)*
   lizards for sand;
Dogs and cats and aardvarks, a mag-*(clap)*
   -nificent band.
And God saw that it was good.

*A*fter all the animals, the *(clap)*
    Lord wasn't through.
He knew there was one more thing He *(clap)*
    wanted to do.
In His image He made man and *(clap)*
    woman, those two.
And God saw that it was good.

Then God blessed those first two folks and *(clap)*
    said, "Look and see.
See the bird and flower. See the *(clap)*
    river and tree.
You shall care for all I've made; Be *(clap)*
    stewards for Me.
It is good. Yes, it is good."

*W*hen the seventh day had dawned, the *(clap)*
    Lord took a rest.
And because He rested then He *(clap)*
    called that day blest.
He had made so much, and all He'd *(clap)*
    made was the best.
It was, oh, so very good.

Sing hallelujah! The Lord God made a world.
Into the darkness His mighty Word He hurled.
And out of nothing creation He unfurled.
And God saw that it was good.

The Lord God Made a World

Traditional American Tune

Carol Greene

Lice

Lice

Patrick Merrick

THE CHILD'S WORLD®, INC.

Library of Congress Cataloging-in-Publication Data
Merrick, Patrick.
Lice / by Patrick Merrick.
p.   cm.
Includes index.
Summary: Describes the physical characteristics,
behavior, habitat, and life cycle of lice,
and how to get rid of them.
ISBN 1-56766-634-5 (lib. bdg. : alk. paper)
1. Pediculosis—Juvenile literature.
2. Lice—Juvenile literature.
[1. Lice.]   I. Title.
RL764.P4M47   1999
616.5'7—dc21   98-45209
                                CIP
                                AC

Photo Credits

ANIMALS ANIMALS © George Bernard: 10
ANIMALS ANIMALS © Raymond A. Mendez: 16
© David M. Budd: 29
© Dr. Chris Hale/Science Photo Laboratory, The National Audubon Society Collection/Photo Researchers: 26
© Mark Clarke/Science Photo Laboratory, The National Audubon Society Collection/Photo Researchers: 24
© Oliver Meckes, The National Audubon Society Collection/Photo Researchers: cover, 2, 15, 19, 20
© Robert and Linda Mitchell: 9, 13, 30
© William E. Ferguson: 6, 23

On the cover...

Front cover: This picture shows what a *human head louse* looks like at 100 times its real size.
Page 2: If you look closely, you can see this human head louse's curved claws.

Table of Contents

School is a wonderful place. It is full of interesting things to learn, see, and do. One of the things you learn about is all of the different animals in nature. In fact, many classrooms have fish, hamsters, birds, or even snakes as pets.

There is one animal, however, that no one wants in school. It is a tiny, fast-moving creature. These animals could attack your teacher, your friends, or even you! What are these creatures? They are lice.

⇐ This human head louse is crawling through someone's hair.

What Do Lice Look Like?

Lice are not really scary creatures. They are just one of nature's animals. The word *lice* is used when there is a group of them. The word *louse* (LOWSS) is used when there is only one.

Lice are part of a group of animals called **insects.** An insect is an animal that has three body parts—a head, a **thorax,** and an **abdomen.** The thorax is the chest of an insect. The abdomen is the insect's stomach area. A louse also has six legs. Each one of a louse's legs ends in a large claw.

Hog lice like this one live on pigs. ⇒

Lice are hard to see because they are very small. In fact, most lice grow to be only one-eighth of an inch long! That is only as big as a sesame seed. The other reason lice are so hard to see is that they are very good at looking like their surroundings. Coloring that helps and animal blend in with its surroundings is called **camouflage.** Lice can be the same color as the hair and skin of the person on whom they are living. Most lice are white, gray, or brown.

⇐ This human head louse blends in with the person's hair.

Where Do Lice Live?

There are different kinds, or **species,** of lice. Some live only on animals. Others live only on people. Different types of lice live in different places on the body.

The best-known type of louse is the *human head louse.* Head lice live in people's hair. They are usually found near the neck or behind the ears. Since head lice live on people, they can be found almost everywhere in the world.

It's easy to see this head louse's body as it sits on someone's hand. ⇒

What Do Lice Eat?

Lice are **parasites.** A parasite is an animal that lives and feeds on another animal. Human head lice and *human body lice* eat only one thing—human blood! They do this by climbing on a person and pushing their needle-like mouths through the person's skin. Then they stay still as they suck up the blood. Lice are very hungry animals. In fact, they can feed as often as six times a day!

You can easily see this *crab louse's* hooked claws. ⇒

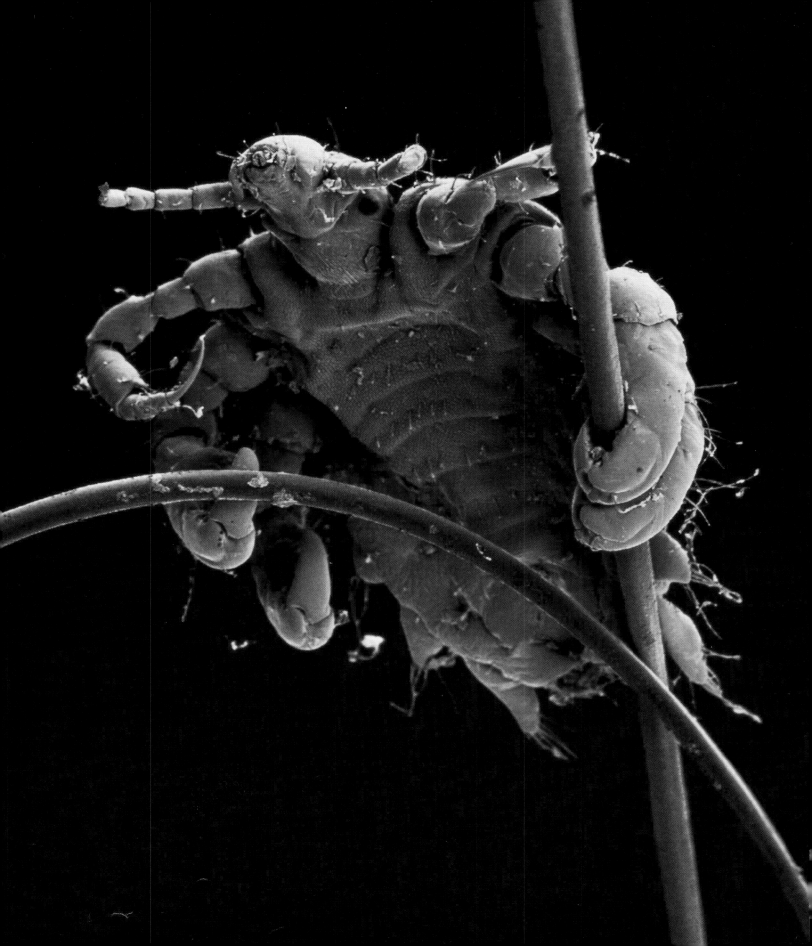

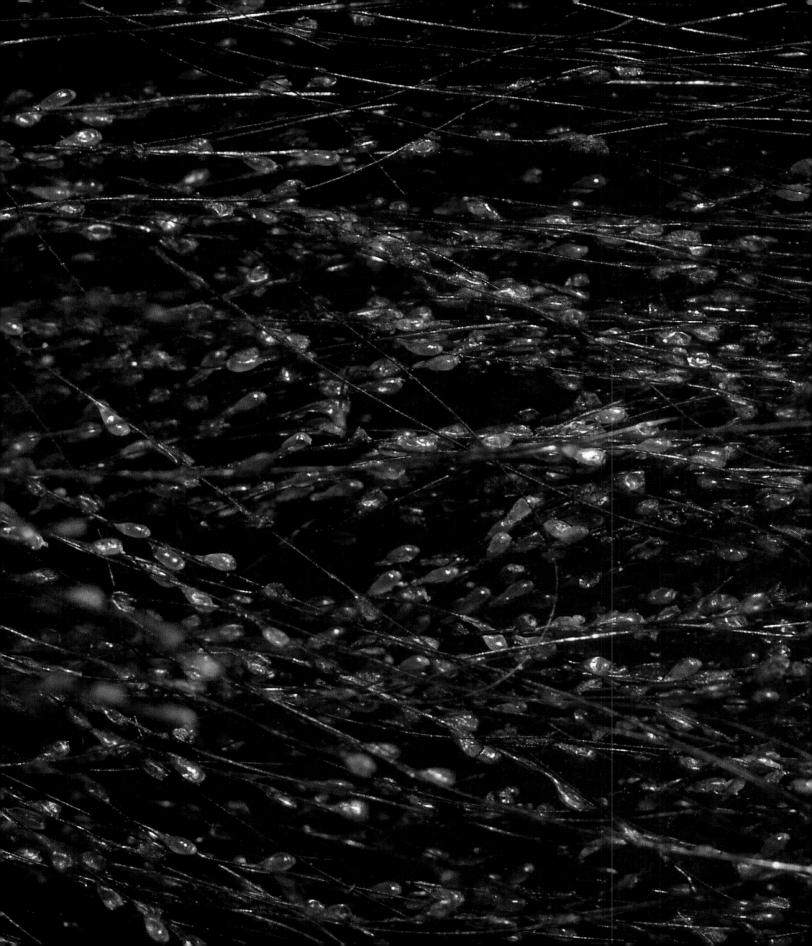

A female louse first finds a **host** animal on which to live. Then she begins to lay eggs. A female louse can live up to one month. Every day she is alive, the female lays eggs. That can add up to 300 eggs!

Lice eggs are called **nits.** Nits are white and very small. As she lays her eggs, the female louse attaches each nit to a strand of hair. After about a week, each egg hatches and a young louse, called a **nymph,** is born. As soon as they are born, nymphs start eating. During the next 10 days, the nymphs slowly change into adult lice. When they are fully grown, the lice mate, and the cycle starts all over again.

Here you can see a nit glued tightly to a piece of hair. ⇒

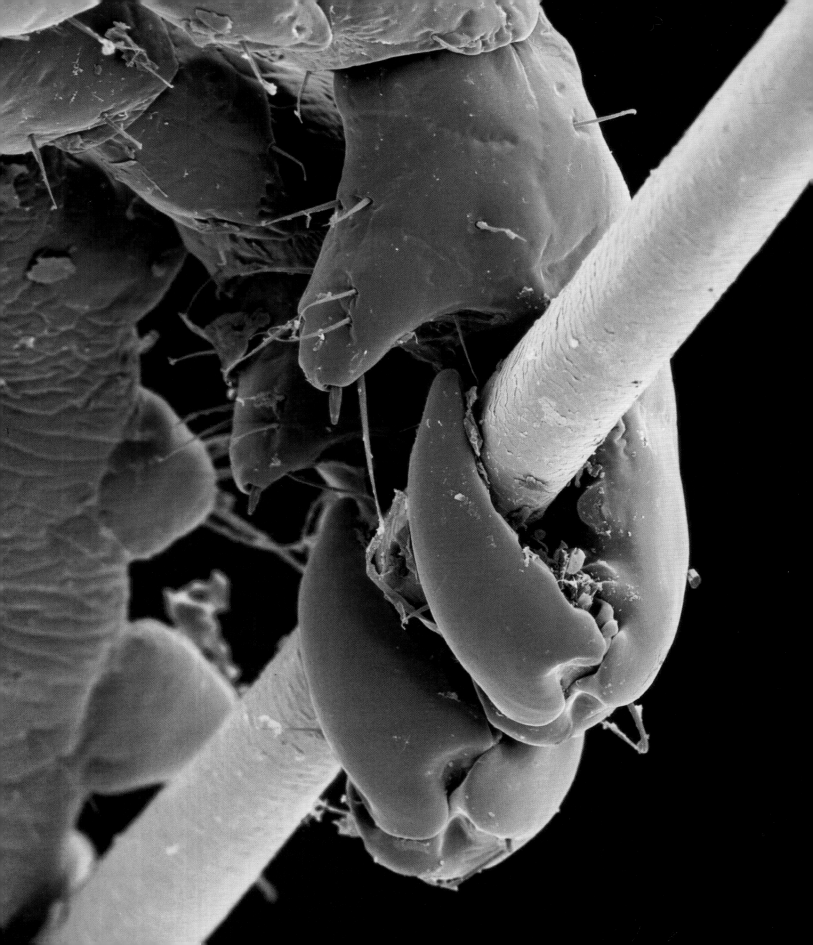

Lice cannot fly or jump. To move around, they use their hooked claws. The claws hold tightly to the hair of the host. But if lice cannot jump, how do they spread to other hosts?

You can get lice only if you touch something that has been in the hair of someone who has lice. Things such as hats, combs and brushes, scarves, and towels can all carry lice. To keep lice out of your hair, never share these things with your friends.

⇐ This crab louse's claw is wrapped tightly around a piece of hair.

Anyone can get lice. Having lice does not mean that you are dirty. It also does not matter if you have long or short hair, or even if you wash your hair every day. In fact, lice are so common that as many as 10 million Americans will get head lice this year.

Head lice like this one can be found on anyone. ⇒

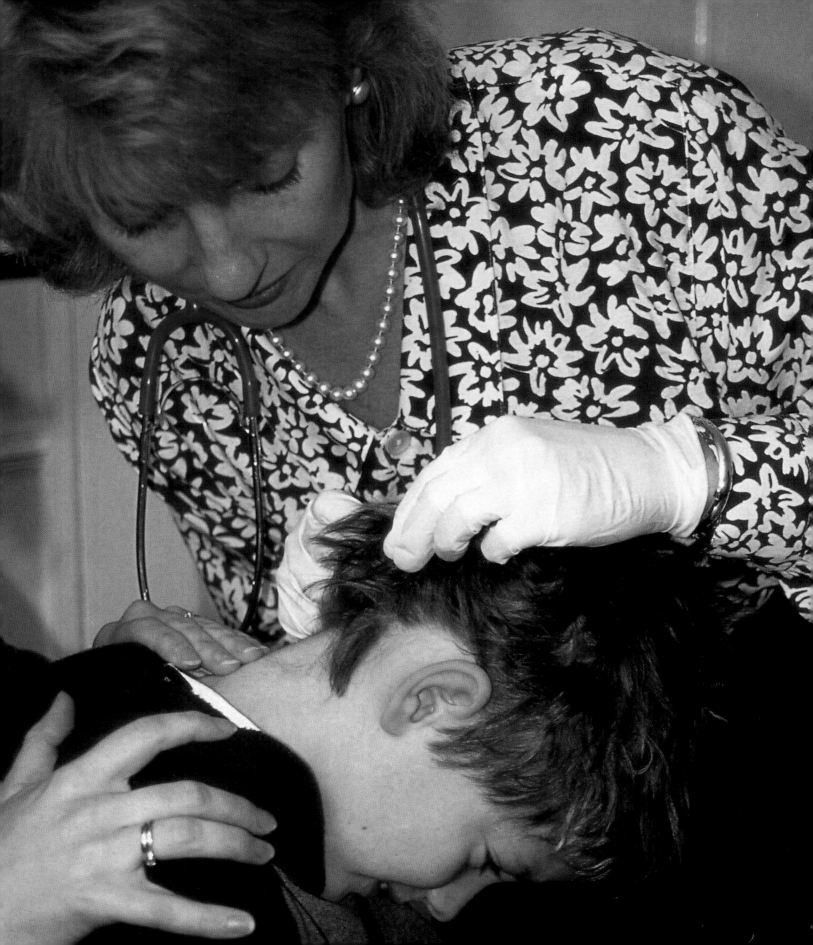

Lice are not dangerous, but they can cause your head to itch. Some people may also get a rash or scratch marks. Even so, these are not usually serious problems. The biggest problem with lice is that it is hard to get rid of them. If you have lice, the first thing you should do is go to see a doctor. The doctor can give you special soaps and shampoos that will kill the lice in your hair and on your clothes.

⇐ This doctor is checking a young boy for head lice.

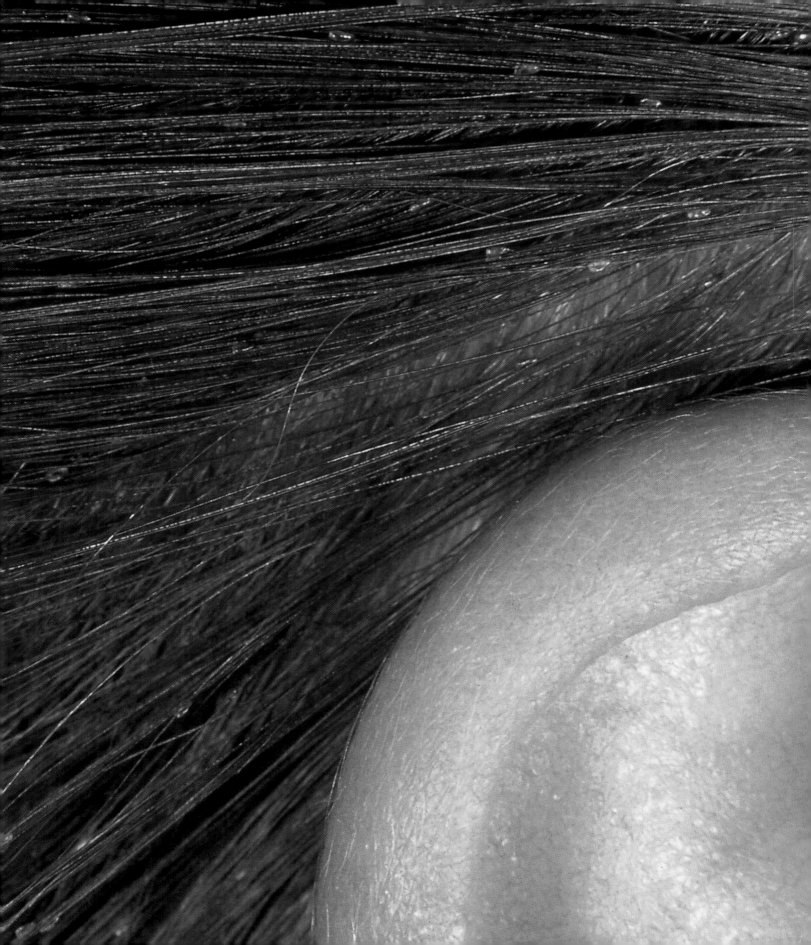

What Can You Do If You Have Lice?

Since lice are hard to see, the easiest way to tell whether you have lice is to have someone look for the nits. If someone can see the nits in your hair, then you have lice. The first thing you should do is check everyone in your family. If one person has lice, others might, too. Next, get a special shampoo made just for getting rid of lice. Wash your hair very well, and then use the special shampoo again in a week. That way, you can be sure you have gotten all of the lice and their eggs.

⇐ You can see the tiny nits in this girl's hair.

Use a *nit comb* to remove all the nits. You might have to use this comb many times. While you are doing this, remember to wash your hats, towels, and pillows in hot water. If you have things that can't be washed, place them in a plastic bag for one week. Without any blood to eat, the lice will die.

The tiny teeth of this nit comb will grab any nits in this boy's hair. ⇒

Finally, remember to tell your teacher or school nurse. Then they can check other students to make sure the lice haven't spread. If you remember not to share combs and hats, you will probably not get lice. If you *do* get lice, simply follow your doctor's directions and you can get rid of them.

Lice are interesting creatures, but they are also one of nature's most annoying pests. If you are careful not to share hats, combs, and other items with other children, you can help stop the spread of lice.

Glossary

abdomen (AB–doh–men)
The abdomen of an insect is its stomach area.

camouflage (KAM–oo–flazh)
Camouflage is coloring or markings that help an animal hide. Lice have camouflage that helps them hide in the hair of people and animals.

host (HOHST)
A host is an animal on which a parasite lives and feeds. People can be hosts to different kinds of lice.

insects (IN–sekts)
An insect is an animal that has a body with three parts. Lice are insects.

nits (NITS)
Nits are lice eggs. Nits are tiny and hard to see.

nymph (NIMF)
When a louse is at the stage of life between nit and adulthood, it is called a nymph.

parasites (PAYR–uh–sites)
Parasites are animals that feed on other animals. Lice are parasites.

species (SPEE–sheez)
A species is a different kind of an animal.

thorax (THOR–ax)
A thorax is the chest of an insect.

Web Sites

Learn more about lice:

http://www.headlice.org

http://www.safe2use.com/pests/lice/history.htm

http://www.ifas.ufl.edu/~insect/urban/human_lice.htm

32

Index